"I HAVE IT ALL"

BETHANY WEBSTER
AND
C. G. COOPER

"I Have It All"

Copyright © 2014 Cooper & Associates. All Rights Reserved

Authors: Bethany Webster and C. G. Cooper
Cover design by Humblenations.com
Editor: Karen Rought

This is a work of fiction. Characters, names, locations and events are all products of the author's imagination. Any similarities to actual events or real persons are completely coincidental.

Any reproduction without the author's consent is strictly prohibited.

TO SEE ALL THE BOOKS
IN THE MENTOR CODE SERIES:
http://www.thementorcode.com/our-books.html

TABLE OF CONTENTS

Chapter 1: The Grind.................... 7

Chapter 2: Unexpected 12

Chapter 3: Have It All?................. 18

Chapter 4: Dreams and Attitude.......... 29

Chapter 5: Law of Attraction 39

Chapter 6: Guilt and Sacrifice............ 48

Chapter 7: Time Manager................ 57

Chapter 8: Guilt at Home................ 64

Chapter 9: Puzzle Pieces................. 72

Chapter 10: Time For Love?.............. 78

Chapter 11: My Time. My Life............ 85

INTRODUCTION

First things first, honey.

This book is a work of fiction. That doesn't mean the nuggets of information offered here are too.

Allow me to explain.

The way I look at it, life experiences teach us best. Second best are the life experiences of others when they're presented as biographies or fables. They're stories of learning, growth and inspiration. These stories serve as kindling for the imagination, spark new ideas, and fire up creative juices. They're like rocket fuel for your success and for your soul.

That's why Carlos and I decided to present my real-life lessons for 'Having It All' in this format.

Whether you're an aspiring entrepreneur, a seasoned veteran of the business world ready to take it to the next level, or a mom like me trying to change your life, it doesn't matter. The principles demonstrated in this story can help take you from where you are right now, to achieving your dreams.

Some of you who know me and know my story—what it took to get me from dead broke to bling-bling, and how my life changed dramatically. Why do I mention this? Because if you know me, you'll no doubt be able to tell the difference between where we took creative license and where we let the facts speak for themselves.

If we haven't met yet, either in person or online, hello! I'm happy to meet you, and can't wait for our paths to cross in real life. Till then, here's what I'm gonna ask you to do: Sit back and enjoy the story, because there's gold in these pages. And if you can find the nuggets... You'll be well on your way to having it all.

Ready to get started? Let's jump right in...

CHAPTER 1
THE GRIND

The ringing of the alarm clock shook me from my dream. The snow-white sands of some far off beach no longer tickled my feet, and the smell of coconut lotion drifted away. It was pitch black in my bedroom. The spot where my husband used to sleep lay cold. I grabbed my folded hospital scrubs and padded to the bathroom.

I groaned as the overhead light flashed on and saw myself in the mirror. My hair was a mess. Hastily tying it back in a ponytail, I ignored my overflowing makeup drawer. No time. There was one stop I had to make before sneaking out of the house.

Dodging the plastic baseball bat, one sneaker and an assortment of army men, I crept into his room. I could just make out his tousled blond hair peaking from beneath the covers. As usual, both feet dangled off the bed.

He looked so peaceful as my eyes adjusted to the night light-illuminated darkness. For a moment I just sat there, watching. My eyes welled up, but I willed away the tears. Every morning was the same. What I wouldn't give to be able to snuggle up next to him and go back to sleep.

Michael was our only son. The doctor said I was lucky. There had been complications during delivery. I couldn't have another child. It made my love for him almost desperate. He was my miracle.

I bent down and kissed him gently on the cheek. He smelled like little boy. Clean and new. My little man. Five going on fifteen. He acted so grown up. He always worried about me.

"I love you," I whispered. Not a sound. He didn't stir. He got that from his father, power sleepers both. We'd been divorced four years.

I backed out of the room and closed the door with a sigh, then checked to make sure the door of the guest room, which now served as my mom's room, was cracked open. It was. Michael always liked to crawl into bed with Grandma. She'd pretend that she was asleep, just like me. It was one of our things.

Snagging a protein bar on my way through the kitchen, I mentally prepared for the day. Another long shift. Another day I wouldn't spend with my little boy. Another day where I should be doing something else.

The thought haunted me as I slipped into my car and backed down the rain slick driveway.

NOTES

NOTES

CHAPTER 2
UNEXPECTED

I had fifteen minutes on break before taking the elevator back up to the third floor. The morning was uneventful so far and I hoped it would stay that way. Working in the Intensive Care Unit (ICU) could be grueling. Long shifts. Sick patients. The occasional heartbreak. Luckily, we had a good staff of doctors and nurses who really cared.

Sitting in the cafeteria, I flipped through the pictures on my phone. More than usual, Michael was on my mind that day. My heart ached at the sight of his smile. He always liked to make funny faces and have me take pictures until he was satisfied that he'd given me his full repertoire. I sighed sadly.

"Is everything okay?" came a voice from my right. I jumped and fumbled with my phone.

I looked around cautiously, hoping it wasn't a former patient or their family. It was always strange seeing patients outside of the ICU. Most were extremely sick and often wanted to talk.

It wasn't a patient who'd asked the question. Squinting through my imperfect vision, I saw that the speaker was a woman, probably in her early sixties, casually dressed, yet...I'm not sure if my description would do her justice. She looked regal in an approachable kind of way.

"Were you talking to me, Ma'am?" I asked.

The woman smiled kindly, stood, walked over, and took the seat across from me. I backed away at her forwardness. I wasn't used to being approached by strangers. It gave me the jitters. There was something familiar about...

"You looked like you were...in pain," she said. "I just thought I'd make sure you were okay."

"Oh," I said. "I was just looking at pictures of my son." I held out my phone and she took it.

"He's a handsome young man," she said as she flipped through the album. "How old is he?"

"He's five."

She nodded and handed the phone back. "You're very lucky. Is he with his father today?"

My face tightened. I was not used to being the one answering questions. As a nurse, I was the caregiver peppering patients and their families with queries. For some reason I answered despite my discomfort. Maybe it was the way she looked at me with such compassion. "No. He's with my mom. His father and I split up a while ago."

She didn't press the point and instead pointed at my name badge. "Busy day up in the ICU, Erika?"

"Not really. I'm sorry, you know my name, but what's…"

"How rude of me. I'm the one who should be sorry, butting in on your morning and whatnot. I am…"

Her words didn't come out before I made the connection, and blurted, "You're Sandra…"

"Please, call me Sandy." Her smile widened.

Sandy was one of the most recognizable figures I knew. A highly successful businesswoman, she'd written the book on starting and growing a multi-million dollar company as a woman. She was a pioneer whose real estate company had more signs around town than anyone I'd ever seen. Her face graced television screens across the country.

"What are you doing here?" I asked, wide-eyed.

"My youngest daughter is about to have her first baby. Just taking a little break from the breathing exercises."

I couldn't believe I was sitting in front of a woman who I'd idolized for years. She was the epitome of a gracious, modern and sophisticated businesswoman. Something I'd wanted to be years ago.

My buzzing phone shattered my stupor. It was the ICU.

"I've gotta run," I said, getting up from the table. "It was so nice meeting you."

Sandy rose and extracted a business card from her pocket. "Here. I'll be around the next couple of days. Give me ring and I'll buy you a cup of coffee."

I took the card reverently and nodded. "Thank you."

NOTES

NOTES

CHAPTER 3
HAVE IT ALL?

We were slammed for the rest of the day, so much so that I didn't have a second to think about my chance encounter with the queen of real estate. It wasn't until I went to change into street clothes that I emptied my scrub pants pockets and her card fell on the floor. I stared at it for a moment, and then slipped it carefully into my purse, still not sure if I'd ever use it.

+++

That night, after Michael fell asleep in my lap in front of the television, I pulled out my laptop. Glancing at Sandy's business card, I typed in her company's web address. The website popped up a second later, and I spent the next hour scouring everything.

She'd had an amazing career. Thirty-five years after getting her real estate license, the company had branches all over the country. The brand exuded professionalism and yet maintained that sense of down home and comfort that home buyers wanted.

I sat tapping the business card on my leg as I stared at the screen. What could it hurt? I would call her the next day.

+++

Sandy was happy that I'd called. She told me that her daughter delivered a healthy baby boy the night before. The entire family was visiting throughout the day so she said she'd have time to sneak out and grab a snack in the cafeteria. I enthusiastically agreed.

The cafeteria wasn't packed for lunch yet, and I easily found Sandy. She sat clacking away at a laptop, the remnants of her snack sitting to the side.

"Good morning!" she said with tired yet happy eyes.

"Thank you so much for meeting with me, Sandy. I know how busy—."

She waved my coming guilt away. "I needed a break. You gave me an excuse to come down and get some coffee. Would you like to get some?"

My time was limited and I was ready to get to know this amazing woman. "No, thanks. I'm set."

"Do you mind if I ask you something?" Sandy questioned as I sat down.

"Um, sure."

Her face turned serious. "You looked a little upset yesterday. Was it because of your son, or something else?"

I sat for a moment, not knowing how to respond. Most of the night before had been spent coming up with questions to ask Sandy. I wanted to learn. I'd had my stint running a small business and craved the secrets. Now she was putting the focus on me. Small, little, insignificant me.

"I just...I'm...it would be nice to have what you have," I blurted, and then cupped my hand over my mouth. My face must have turned red. Sandy just smiled.

"And what do you think I have?"

I searched for the right words, feeling flustered at the thought of offending her again. "You have it all."

Sandy chuckled lightly. "And why do you think that is?"

I shrugged. "You just seem so at peace." I motioned to her outfit. "You've been up all night and you still look fabulous."

She laughed at that.

Taking a deep breath, I said, "You're obviously successful, and I can tell that you love your family." I could. It was one of those things that women instinctively knew about other women. "I wish I had that."

Sandy nodded. "Would you like me to tell you a story?"

"Yes."

"Okay. You're right. Today I have everything I want, a prosperous business, a wonderful family and a fulfilling life. It wasn't always like this. Thirty-five years ago I was a new mother without a career. I'd gone to college, but hadn't done anything with my degree. My husband made enough money that I could stay home and prepare for motherhood. We had a good life. Our first son was wonderful, and I'll always cherish those first months. But a strange thing happened the day he turned six-months-old. I was pushing his stroller through the neighborhood when I saw a real estate agent placing a For Sale sign in a yard. The man was probably in his late fifties, and he was having a hard time getting it pushed into the dirt. I walked over and offered to help. Together we got it in. He thanked me and gave me his card. The sight of it sent my mind swirling to the past. My father was a real estate investor for the majority of his life. Growing up, I spent weekends driving around the city helping him find houses to buy. He always called me his first assistant.

"Well, I'd never thought about going into real estate until that moment, standing in front of that new For Sale sign. Instead of going home, I walked with my newborn all the way to the library—it must've been four miles—and asked the librarian for information on becoming a real estate agent. An hour later, I left with a crying baby and an armful of copied pages. I was ecstatic. My husband wasn't. He told me that he worked hard to give me the opportunity to stay at home. At first, I was disappointed. Then I got angry. I wanted to be a mom AND a businesswoman. That fire only got hotter.

"So, without him knowing it, I started taking a real estate correspondence course. I paid for it with some money I'd been saving for a new couch.

Two-months later, I took and passed the state real estate exam. Bill, my husband, sat blank-faced when I told him. The only thing he said as he got up from the dinner table was, "As long as it doesn't interfere with the baby." I made myself the promise that it wouldn't. That wasn't to be."

"Why not?" I asked. Nothing in her bio had said anything about struggling in the beginning. Then again, why would you openly admit to that?

"I had to start at the bottom, making calls to get listings and helping other agents, but pretty soon I was signing new clients on my own. Everything I'd learned from my father came in handy. It turned out that even though I wasn't a veteran real estate agent, my past experience evaluating property gave me an edge. Pretty soon I was in demand. Within a year I'd somehow become the office's rising star. Unfortunately, the long hours I put in took away from my time at home. It didn't slow from there. I threw myself into work, despite the looks from my husband. After my first sale, I put our son in a part-time daycare. That soon turned into full-time. He was well cared for, but the guilt still gnawed at me.

"By my third year, I was closing in on six-figures. I had an assistant and more than one other agent wanted to be on my team. The money was great, but the hours were long. It didn't help that most of my showings were at night and on the weekends. Needless to say, my family life suffered. I didn't know how to juggle them both."

I could sympathize. My nursing career meant being on-call on nights and weekends. "How long did that go on?"

Sandy shrugged. "Unfortunately, too long. I can admit that ambition got the best of me. Once I'd had a taste of success, I wanted more. It's wasn't enough to make extra spending money. I wanted to show my husband, and everyone else, that I could be a good mom and a successful businesswoman. Don't get me wrong; I don't regret the sacrifices. I just think I could've been a little smarter about it. My motivation stemmed from a bit of bitterness, too."

"What changed?" I knew she'd started her company at some point. How had she figured it all out?

"Three years after getting my real estate license, I left my first company and started a new brokerage. I was working longer and longer hours trying to recruit and sell at the same time. It was tough <u>and</u> rewarding. As I made more money, my husband scaled back on his own work. We did our best to stay flexible for our growing family. By then I'd had my daughter. Sometimes I look back and wonder how we did it. I tell you these things not to complain or brag, but so you can see that although I have it all now, it took time getting here."

"Thank you for telling me. I guess sometimes it's simpler to assume that others had it easy. I guess nothing worthwhile comes that way." I tried to sound confident, but to my ears the words came out lamely.

Sandy patted my arm. "It's not all bad. If I didn't go through all the hard times, there is no way I could fully enjoy where I am now. Do you know what I mean?"

"I do. It's just, I don't…"

"Why don't you take a couple days to figure out what your life would look like if you had it all. Write it down. What would your world look like? Make your description vivid and memorable. You should be able to shut your eyes and picture it."

I nodded and took a sip of my coffee, my mind already wandering down a familiar path.

PRACTICE

Describe what your perfect life would look like. Be specific. Tell your future story. Here are some questions that may help mold your vision:

- Where would you live?
- What would you do to make money?
- Who would you hang out with?
- What would your family look like?
- Where would you go on vacation?
- How much money would you make every month, every year?
- What would it feel like to get there?

NOTES

NOTES

CHAPTER 4
DREAMS AND ATTITUDE

That night I sat down and did as Sandy had instructed. I wrote down my dreams. I described time with my son, running on the beach, making enough money to support our travels, finding a man to spend the rest of my life with, running a successful business...

The thoughts and words flowed until I sat panting, out of breath, weak from the effort. A part of my soul felt like it had flown out of my body and onto the lined sheet of paper. I stared at what I had written as if someone else had scribbled it down. It had been so long since I'd allowed myself to dream that it felt like a long lost friend coming home at last. Warm and inviting.

I don't cry easily, but that night the tears came. They were happy tears. As I went about the next day, more revelations made themselves known. It was as if I'd been living with half of my senses. Colors looked more vibrant. Smells more enticing. Textures tickled my skin.

And it had all happened because, for the first time in ages, I'd allowed the inner me to come out and play. It was like being a child again, when everything was shiny and new. How had I lived without it? I'd stuck myself in a box, shut off from the world, too afraid, or maybe just too stubborn to peek out.

Work flew by as I made it a point to smile and be grateful for my coworkers and patients. It didn't take long for someone to notice.

"What are you so cheery about?" came the verbal slap from Martha, one of my coworkers. She was known for her cutting jabs. She lorded over us through intimidation and snark. Upper management knew her as a royal pain. More than a few new hires had left their first day in tears thanks to Martha's reign. I did my best to avoid her. As I stared at her that day, I didn't see a confident woman. I saw a bitter girl who'd made a decision to throw her lot back at the world instead of changing her own. I knew in that instant that it was the same person I would have become if I hadn't met Sandy.

With the biggest genuine smile I could muster, I said, "Just having a wonderful day, Martha. How are you?"

She stood in shocked silence. We'd worked together for three years, but I'd never had the courage to stand up to her, let alone be nice in the face of her tyranny. I smiled innocently and went on my way, leaving her to contemplate my new attitude.

At lunch, I told Sandy what had happened. She laughed in delight. "The power of a positive attitude never ceases to amaze me. Have you ever noticed how one bad apple can spoil a bunch?"

I nodded. I'd seen it many times. Sometimes it was a fellow staff member who was having a "bad day" or a patient's husband who couldn't help being a pest because they were "taking care" of their loved one. I was guilty of it too, snapping at my mom all too often after a long day at work.

"How did your assignment go?" asked Sandy.

Fighting past the lump in my throat, I pulled out the list from my purse and handed it to her. Never in my life had I shared my dreams with anyone. Not even my ex. I waited nervously for her to finish reading. A moment later she looked up, a slight shimmer in her eye.

"How did it feel writing this down?"

"Like it was long overdue."

Sandy smiled. "Do you know how many people never take the time to write down what they want, their hopes and dreams? Once you put it on paper, your dream has a chance of coming true. It took me a long time to realize that. Once I did, goals became minor road blocks and dreams blossomed into reality. Now, I'm not saying it doesn't take hard work, because it does. That being said, I don't see anything on this list that isn't achievable as long as you put in the time and effort."

I nodded my understanding, waiting anxiously to hear how I would get there.

Sandy looked down at the handwritten note again. "It says here that you want to run a successful business." A grin stretched. "I might be able to help you with that."

My heart leapt at the comment.

"Really?"

"I promised you I would help, and I will. I'll help you under two conditions." Here it was, the loophole, the catch. "One, you must listen, and two, you must implement what I tell you to do as if your life depended on it. It's not my ego talking when I say that I am very good at what I do. It took a lot of trial and error to get to this point, but even though you'll make some mistakes along the way, and believe me you will, you can learn from my blunders and will hopefully be able to sidestep them. So what do you say, would you like me to help?"

For a moment, I couldn't open my mouth. Here was this wonderful woman who, before a few days ago, had never known me. She was not only reaching out, teaching me lessons that she could probably sell for thousands, if not millions of dollars, but she was giving me hope. That, more than anything, was what I wanted, what I needed, desperately.

"Sandy, I would love your help."

"Great! Let's talk a little more about attitude. I love how you reacted to your coworker. It shows that you have a good heart, a willingness to be kind. That's important. I'm sure you've found that being nice to someone can be extremely rewarding."

I had. "There are a lot of nurses and techs who punch a clock, rarely spending the extra time with patients. It's like they're hollow. The best ones give a piece of themselves to the work."

"Then you're ahead of ninety five percent of the rest of the human race. You recognize the value of being genuine, kind and helpful. That's what becoming a success is all about: attitude. If you walk around with a chip on your shoulder, brushing people off, being fake, do you think people will want to do business with you?"

"Of course not," I said, enjoying the depth of what she was saying.

"If I had a dime for every real estate agent who..." She stopped herself. "Never mind. I'd rather we focus on the positive. In my world, the top agents know how to take care of clients. You might've seen these reality TV shows where real estate agents act like they're God's gift to the industry." I nodded. Those personalities were the antithesis of how I wanted to do business. "We don't allow that in our firm. Attitude comes first. I can work with someone with a positive outlook. A person's attitude not only affects their business, but it affects everyone around them. Like I said before, a cynical attitude poisons the air, and it pollutes our chances of finding happiness."

PRACTICE

Success begins inside you. In order to achieve that which you desire, repairing your passion and your attitude comes first. Imagine riding a bike with no wheels or building a house without a foundation. It won't work.

It's the same for people. How can you build and run a successful enterprise without first taking a look in the mirror? Yes, you can start down the path, but at some point you will stumble.

Write down all the things in your life that are dragging you down and stealing your passion. It may be a pessimistic attitude, negative friends, poor diet or a horrible work place. Be honest. Don't complain just to complain. Examine all aspects of your personal, professional and spiritual life. Where are you lacking? What parts of your attitude could you repair?

The second part of your assignment starts tomorrow. From the moment you wake, be ever conscious of your thoughts and emotions. The nanosecond a negative thought comes to mind (it's too early, my back is sore, my husband is snoring...) purge it from your life. Turn it into something positive (the sunrise is beautiful at this hour, I think I'll go for a run today, I love my husband...).

Attitude starts with the smallest things. If you start the day by letting a cold cup of coffee or a burnt piece of toast ruin your attitude, what will happen when something really bad happens? The loss of an employee? A lawsuit? The death of a loved one?

The most successful people in the world constantly focus on their attitude and the attitudes of those around them. They surround themselves with those who will ensure success while challenging and contributing to the team. A team member with a bad attitude is like a dormant cancer waiting to infect.

NOTES

NOTES

CHAPTER 5
LAW OF ATTRACTION

Sandy would be out of town for the next week, so I had all that time to focus on what we had already talked about. I spent my days working and being mindful of my outlook. Little disturbances like a crabby patient or slow lab work sometimes threatened to invade my clarity. I resisted by staying positive.

It just so happened that during that week I got a chance to hang out with some friends after work. I didn't get to do it often, due to my job and Michael, but I went when I could. Seeing old friends provided a nice distraction.

It started off innocently enough. We mingled and snacked. Helen, our hostess, was talking about her husband, telling stories, making us laugh. Suddenly, in my mind, I took a step back. A feeling of unease sent chills down my arms. I was the only one not laughing. Helen noticed.

"What is it, Erika? You look like you saw a ghost." Everyone giggled. My face went hot.

"I'm sorry, I...I have to go," I said.

I made it to the front door before Helen caught up to me, a look of concern on her face. "Are you okay, Erika? Is it Michael?"

The sound of my son's name gave me strength. "I really am sorry. I didn't mean to interrupt. It's just..." I tried to find the right words. "It's just that I don't know if I feel comfortable being around when you're talking about your husband that way."

Her eyes went wide, then narrowed appraisingly, a guffaw bursting from her mouth. "When did you get to be such a square?"

Rather than answer, I turned and left.

+++

Two days later, Sandy and I had our next meeting; she looking business-like and beautiful, me trying my best to put on a brave face. Since leaving Helen's house, I'd struggled to maintain my positive attitude. Her dismissal by calling me 'a square' played over and over in my head. Maybe she was right.

"How was your trip?" I asked, wanting to get right to business, to distract my frazzled mind.

"Busy, but very productive. I had a chance to work with a group of new agents. It was a lot of fun and one of the things I enjoy most now that I'm not actively selling homes. What about you? How was your week?"

I contemplated not telling her about the episode at Helen's, but when I looked into her inquisitive eyes, I knew I had to. She listened as I retold the story.

"Why did it upset you?" she asked.

I shook my head, trying to shake the answer free. "I'm not sure. All I know is that what she was saying really upset me, and I don't understand why."

Sandy smiled. "I do."

I looked up from my coffee. "You do?"

She nodded. "How long have you known those women?"

"For years."

"Would you say they're close friends?"

"As close as I have."

"During these get-togethers, do they spend a lot of time talking about their husbands or gossiping about other people?"

"Maybe."

"Think back to what Helen was saying when you got upset. Was she making fun of her husband in a mean-spirited way?"

I thought back to that moment. Helen was always saying things 'in jest,' but you always had that nagging feeling... "Maybe?"

"Let me tell you something I learned from one of my mentors. Jokes are a funny thing, but they're often a mask for something else. Have you ever heard comedians say that a great joke is funny because it has an element of truth to it?"

That's when the light turned on in my head.

Sandy continued. "I think the reason Helen's joke disturbed you was because she delivered a thinly veiled accusation against her husband. She was airing her husband's dirty laundry in front of her friends."

"That's what it was. When I realized what she was doing, I felt totally uncomfortable. I know her husband, and he is a really nice guy. He doesn't deserve her talking behind his back." Even as I said it, I knew I'd done the same thing in the past, maybe even with my ex-husband.

"We're all guilty of it," said Sandy. "The moment I realized my own wrongdoings, I turned the tables. Now, most of my jokes are on me."

I liked that idea.

"So, what should I do about Helen?"

"That's up to you. It depends on how close you are. If she's a good friend, you may want to mention something, tactfully. Just say that you're trying to be better about keeping positive, and that talking about other people, even in jest, makes you uncomfortable. If she's only an acquaintance or she brushes you off, you may want to consider not spending time with her. That's up to you."

I sat, thinking. Sure, Helen was fun to be around, but now that I'd had time to think about the episode, I wondered if she said things about me behind my back.

"I'll think about it," I said.

Sandy nodded. "Have you heard of the law of attraction?"

"You mean about how what you want most you tend to get?"

"Exactly. You're at a crucial crossroads. You need to decide what you want most. Do you want to be around positive and successful people, or do you want negative Nancys pulling you down?

Once you start along the path to your dreams, there will be passion thieves—friends, family members and total strangers who want to keep you from climbing the mountain of success. Take a look at who you're spending time with. Are they supportive? Are they positive? Will they help or hinder your journey? Countless would-be success stories get crushed by a bad crowd. You need to decide whether your vision of the future is worth restructuring your life."

PRACTICE

Take a look around. Who do you spend time with? Is Bob in the cubicle next to you always cutting others down? Is your sister constantly complaining about her kids and husband?

How are their actions affecting you? Do you cower when Bob enters the office? Do you sit and listen to your sister as she rattles on about her horrible life?

If you think they aren't affecting you in some way, you're wrong. Successful professionals surround themselves with positive and success-oriented acquaintants.

Analyze your life. See what changes you can make within your circle of friends. This may be a hard decision, but just like a drug addict trying to kick his habit, you have to stay out of situations that will only bring you down. Life's too short and success is calling.

NOTES

NOTES

CHAPTER 6
GUILT AND SACRIFICE

With Sandy's support, I revived the little business I'd run out of my home before getting divorced. There had always been an excuse for not starting again: Michael, work, no time. I vowed to treat it differently, more professionally.

As I got reacquainted with my products and dusted off old materials, I thought about what Sandy had said about who I spent time with. With work and Michael, there wasn't much time left. Those extra hours were typically spent in front of the television or the rare visit with ladies in the neighborhood. Most were nice, but I didn't know them well. There would be time to reach out and make new friends.

Helen was another story. The same day I talked to Sandy, I made the dreaded phone call. I explained how I'd felt the night of the party, trying hard not to point the finger at her, instead focusing on my personal quest to be better.

"You're kidding, right?" Helen laughed.

I exhaled. "No, I'm not."

"Well that's just ridiculous. Everyone else knows I was kidding. I don't know why you have to take it so seriously."

I imagined Sandy standing next to me, prodding me, and the thought gave me courage. "Maybe I'm just not explaining it properly, but it's how I feel."

"Whatever. Just let me know if you change your mind."

"Thanks, I will," I said, instantly making the decision that unless Helen changed her ways, she wouldn't be a part of my life. Rather than feel sad, I felt relief. I'd made the hard call, and probably lost of friend, but my gut told me I was free.

I got back to work, reinvigorated, anxious to purge my old life and step forward with the new.

+++

Over the next few days, I worked hard to get my business up and running. I reached out to old contacts and made a list of new prospects. Despite being at home, I didn't get to see Michael much. My mom threw me the occasional dirty look, judging the way I spent my after-hours. She'd never believed in my business, saying it was a waste of time and that it kept me from my family. She thought having a full-time job was sufficient.

That thought crept in, threatening to unbalance my resolve. By the time I sat across from Sandy in the hospital cafeteria, I'm sure you could see my shoulders drooping from the amount of guilt I was carrying.

Sandy noticed right away and asked, concerned. I told her about the time I'd spent getting my business out of its old cardboard box, and the feelings of guilt over not spending more time with my son.

"That's only natural. You're starting over. Tell me, is there any other time you have to grow your business?"

There wasn't. "No. After work and on the weekend is all I have."

"And you're still serious about moving forward, growing your business from the ground up?"

I felt the tears threatening to trickle. "I do want it, but I just want to make sure I'm being smart."

Sandy's eyes softened. "Do you think I would tell you to do something I haven't done? Of course not. Look, part of growing a business and having a home life means sacrifice. Now, more than ever, you're going to have to keep your eyes forward, never forgetting your dream. Did you know that guilt is the number one killer of dreams?"

I shook my head, still fighting back my emotions.

"It is. Guilt is sneaky. It seeps in slowly and fills you before you know it's there. And it's everywhere. It comes from all sides. Your goals have to be powerful enough to ward off the guilt and tug you forward, allowing you to burst across the finish line."

"How did you do it?" I asked, wanting desperately to throw off the chains that still threatened to hold me down.

"It wasn't easy for me either. Having a family makes it even harder. I had to retrain myself. Instead of thinking about why I couldn't or shouldn't do something, I stopped listening to the excuses in my head. What made you stop running your business before?"

My shoulders slumped. "My ex and I were going through our divorce and I was a mess. I cut back on anything that wasn't work or my son."

"Was their any guilt involved?"

"Yes. I was so worried about spending time with Michael that I probably smothered him with love. My conscience kept telling me to quit my dream because of the divorce. I listened."

"That's okay. We all go through bad times. Yours just happened to be divorce. What you didn't know at the time, and it's not your fault, is that if you keep your eyes on the prize, and not allow the excuses to get to you, you can press through any catastrophe. At that point your dream *is* your safe place. It's like a warm blanket. You go to it in good times and bad. I lost my mother five years into building my company. We were very close. It was sudden and it almost crushed me. Other than my family, do you know what kept me going?"

"Your business?" I said.

"Yes. Not only did it keep me busy, it filled a part of the hole left by my mother's passing. A piece of her was still with me, and I used it to work harder. That's when I learned another lesson. Guilt can go the other way, too. As some point, when your business expands, you'll feel guilty saying no to customers or partners. After my mother's death, I dove into my business head first. It helped, but it also hurt. I didn't want to turn a client away or say no to a weekend showing. Pretty soon my home life suffered more than before. I never saw my kids or my husband. It put a strain on my marriage that took time to repair. So you see, guilt threatens at every turn. It pushes and pulls. It's enticing and tricks us into believing that we have to change course or our world will fall apart.

"Finding the right balance and keeping our eyes on the prize is crucial. Remember, your dream, just like mine, is to have a successful business <u>and</u> be a great mom. Every decision you make will affect both roles. It's sometimes easier for singles because they really only have themselves to worry about. If they want to eat peanut butter and jelly sandwiches every day, that's okay. You and I have to go home and take care of the family, make dinner, show emotion and give our love."

I appreciated the way Sandy brought family into the picture. She understood my struggle. She'd walked the walk. I wanted it so badly, I could taste it. It was time to shut out the guilt and get to work.

PRACTICE

How has guilt derailed your life? Is it, even now, threatening to bring you down and hold you back, telling you to forget your dreams and stay in the same place, static?

Write down the things that are making you feel guilty. Is it that you're spending too much time away from home? Are you spending too little time on your business?

Once you have what makes you feel guilty written down, turn them into positive outlooks like, "If I spend more time on my business, I can spend more time with my family later," or, "If I'm smart about the time I spend on my business, I'll have more time with my family."

Everyone is different. Find what triggers your guilt and work to ignore it when it rears its ugly head.

NOTES

NOTES

CHAPTER 7
TIME MANAGER

"How well do you manage your time?" asked Sandy.

"What do you mean?"

"Are you a good time manager? Does it ever feel like you're running behind, or like you're flying by the seat of your pants, not knowing what comes next?"

My face flushed. I was always running behind. It'd become sort of a joke with my friends. "All the time. Between work, my business and Michael, sometimes I feel like I don't have time to eat."

Sandy smiled. "It's only going to get worse. Do you have a calendar?"

"Well, sometimes I put stuff in my phone to remind me of doctor appointments and things."

"I said things are going to get worse. What I meant to say was that you're going to get busier. If you're going to juggle a son, a full-time job and a business, you have to be serious about time management. If you don't know what's happening from hour to hour, you end up wasting time instead of using it to your benefit. Your time is <u>your</u> time. Be stingy with it. Don't give it up without a fight. When I first started in real estate, I wasted whole days because I was disorganized. A prospect would call and I'd drop everything to see them. Someone wanted to see one of my listings, and I hopped in my car to open the property, instead of scheduling a time for later. I ran myself ragged, until a veteran agent finally pulled me aside and showed me how to run my schedule."

It sounded good, but I hadn't used a calendar since high school. "Where do I start? I feel like my days are a mess of things and no two are ever the same."

"Start with the little things. You have to eat and sleep, right?"

I laughed. "Of course. Isn't that a little nitpicky? You want me to schedule time to eat and sleep?"

"I know it sounds silly, but if you're serious about being successful, mapping out your day is a must. How does it make you feel when you're late or you miss an appointment?"

That was easy. It'd happened the weekend before when I'd forgotten about a birthday party Michael was supposed to go to. "Embarrassed."

"Okay. How about when you don't know what's happening day-to-day, week-to-week?"

Another easy one. "It makes me crazy. I feel like I spend my time trying to remember something I forgot, like I'm playing catch-up."

"How would it make you feel if you knew exactly what was supposed to happen every single day?"

I couldn't imagine. I'd gotten so used to the feeling of being disorganized that the thought of having a firm handle on my routine seemed foreign. "I don't know. I'm embarrassed to admit that I've kind of always been a little scattered. I was almost late to my own wedding!"

We both laughed at that. "Well that's not good. It sounds like we need to change your mindset. I recommend starting with a paper organizer. It doesn't have to be fancy, but it needs to have your days broken down into fifteen minute increments."

The thought of going to that extreme frightened me. I didn't want to be chained to a schedule.

Sandy continued. "I like to have plenty of room to take notes. That way, if I'm with a client or a new agent, I can jot things down in my calendar and refer back to it if needed. Your calendar should be like your Bible. It needs to be with you at all times, and you must commit to it. If you don't place that much importance on your time, other people won't either. The moment I started guarding my time, and only scheduling meetings when they were convenient for me, things changed drastically. The choke-hold was gone. I could breathe easy knowing all my tasks were being completed, and that I was taking care of myself and my family."

"What about emergencies?"

"You can't really schedule for emergencies, but having a schedule allows you to reschedule when needed. Trust me, if I have to miss a day, there's a lot of rearranging to do, but that's okay. At least I know when I'll have time for rescheduled meetings."

It was hard to believe that Sandy had ever been disorganized. Sitting across from me, she looking like the model of composure. What she was telling me meant that I would not only have to change my habits, I'd also have to change my way of thinking. I thought I'd guarded my time, at least with Michael, but it turned out that I really wasn't doing it right. I needed to put my foot down, declare that my time was <u>my</u> time.

PRACTICE

If you're serious about success, time management must be one of your strongest skills. It's easy to get pulled in a thousand different directions. The problem is that you don't have a thousand hours in a day.

If you're not already using one, buy an organizer or use one on your smart phone/computer. Depending on how far you've fallen off the time management wagon, you may need to be extremely detailed with scheduling: listing the times you eat, sleep, spend time with family, meditate, pray, read, work out, etc.

Get started now. Pull out your calendar, and map out the coming week.

NOTES

NOTES

CHAPTER 8
GUILT AT HOME

Sandy was gone for another two weeks, so that left me with the task of organizing my life. I quickly found that knowing when and where I was supposed to be, not vaguely but specifically, made me sleep better at night. Before, I'd felt nervous thinking I was forgetting something. The funny thing was that my personal life suddenly mimicked my nursing career.

Every patient had a strict schedule for examinations, medications and rehab. I had run their calendars for years not realizing I should've done the same for myself. I laughed at the epiphany. There was an organized professional living inside me!

It took a few days to get in the routine of using my organizer. Understanding how long certain tasks took, and leaving a little buffer time in between events helped me from pulling out my hair those first two weeks. I got my time back.

My side business picked up. Now that I knew when to work at it, I got into a routine, scheduling time for busy work and time for prospecting. Pretty soon I was on a roll. I was more productive than I'd ever been because I knew I had a finite amount of time to do what needed to be done.

Once I knew when it was time to work, and when it was time to play, I was able to spend quality time with Michael. I put my phone away, shut my professional brain, and immersed myself in his giggly little world. My mood improved and so did my mom's. I hadn't realized how much my lack of organization had affected her. She was there to help, but she had a life, too.

I apologized to her when my thoughtlessness smacked me in the face.

"It's okay, honey," she said. "I'm just glad you're pulling it all together. You seem...better."

Her words struck me. Had I been that unhappy? Had it been so obvious? I was ashamed that I'd let my gloominess touch those around me.

The same night I apologized to my mom, Michael surprised me by complaining about the time I was spending 'working.' He'd never said anything before. I asked him how he felt, and in a voice that only a five year old can use, he said, "I'm mad at you, Mommy." He stomped off to his room, leaving me standing in shocked silence.

His attitude continued to sour over the coming days. It made me sad and frustrated. I was trying so hard. We played together almost every night. <u>What am I doing wrong?</u> I asked myself.

By the time my next meeting with Sandy came around, I was frantic. Michael's finger pointing was starting to have an effect on me. I felt like I was walking on eggshells every time I stepped into the house. Something had to change.

+++

I told Sandy about Michael, feeling like all I was doing was dumping on the poor woman.

"Have you told him <u>why</u> you have to work?" asked Sandy.

"I've told him that we have to have money to buy food and pay for the house. Is that what you mean?"

"No. I mean, have you told him about your dreams. Have you shown him what you're building for the two of you?"

"I...I don't know. I may have mentioned something at some point," I said.

"How does it make you feel when he says those things to you?"

"Well, I know he's just a little boy, but it hurts. It makes me feel like I'm doing something wrong. It makes me feel guilty for..."

"Aha! You said it makes you feel guilty. See? Even if you're doing things right, the guilt creeps in. Has it affected your business?"

I thought back to the previous nights, remembering on more than one occasion not being totally focused on what I was doing. "Yes."

"Okay. So it's important that we make that feeling of guilt go away, right?"

"Uh huh."

"You said that Michael is just a little boy. I had a little boy. Kids are smarter than we think. They pick up on things we don't. Do you think he likes to see you happy?"

"Of course."

"Do your dreams make you happy?"

"Yes," I said, smiling.

"You need to share that with him. Tell him why you're doing what you're doing. Let him be part of the process. Let him encourage you. Let him come along for the ride. It's good for him and for you. You should probably do the same with your mother. Let her know what you've been up to. I learned early on that if you don't have your family on board, your chances of success are greatly diminished. It's like having a baseball team with only half the players on the field. You're severely crippled in your efforts."

"What if they don't understand? What if they think I'm wrong?"

Sandy smiled. "They don't have to understand everything, but they do have to understand why you're doing it. You're like me. You're not just in it for the acclaim. You want to provide for your family. You want the freedom to spend more time with them, to take them on vacations. Go back to your dreams sheet. Explain the why behind each dream. Even better, make a vision board. Get a cork board or poster board. Cut out pictures from magazines or print pictures you find online that represent your dreams and pin or paste them up. Let your son be part of that."

"I can do that," I said, wondering what my mom would say.

PRACTICE

A lot of professionals and business owners fail because they don't have support from their family. Don't be one of them.

Share your dreams with your family. They're already a part of your dream, so let them be an active part. Let your kids write down their own dreams. Use a vision board. Kids love that. It lets them "see" what you're dreaming. A new house? A vacation? A day off? Hear what your spouse/significant other wants. There's nothing better than a family chasing dreams together.

NOTES

NOTES

CHAPTER 9
PUZZLE PIECES

That night I sat Michael down and described my dreams, told him why I was building my business. He sat, listening, acting like a big boy. I bit my lip, stifling a laugh at his earnestness.

Finally, after a minute of thinking, he said, "Mommy, is it okay for me to have dreams, too?"

I hugged him and said, "Of course, sweetie. Why don't we do that right now?"

It was wonderful having him next to me, dreaming many of the same dreams. We giggled and high-fived as I wrote down what he wanted. I pulled out some old magazines, and we cut out the images that represented our dreams. Some were trivial, like a toy he'd seen on TV. Other ideas went deeper. Michael cut out a picture of a mom, dad and son, adding it to our vision board.

Later, he sat on the floor, doing 'work' as I polished a follow-up email to a potential customer. I even let Michael press send.

Things got better. Then, over the next weeks, I started leaving before his bedtime for training and sales meetings. In his head, it was okay if I worked at home, but going away didn't fit into his plan.

I tried to explain it the same way I had with the dreams, but something about the physical act of me leaving the house brought out the stubborn five-year-old in him. We endured teary goodbyes as the absences increased in frequency. I was a nervous wreck the hour before departing, and truth be told, I was probably less than effective in my meetings knowing he was home wanting me with him.

Sandy was on an extended working vacation with her family, so I decided to send her an email, quickly outlining the issue. Maybe she had a solution. Surprisingly, minutes later, she called.

"Hi, Erika! How's the weather at home?"

"We got a little rain yesterday, but it's been pretty warm."

"Great. So what's going on with your son?"

I explained Michael's behavior, wondering out loud what could be done.

"Believe it or not, this one may be easier to fix than you think. I have a friend who taught me a great tactic back when I was showing properties at odd hours. My kids hated it when I left. Like you, I felt horrible. It was like I was abandoning my children. This saved me. Here's what you do. Buy a big piece of poster board. Find out what Michael really wants. For my son it was a BB gun. My daughter wanted a dollhouse. Draw those things on the poster board together. Keep the price within reason. You shouldn't have to spend more than a couple hundred dollars on what they want. Now, cut the poster board up into pieces. Every time you leave to work on your business, let him put up one of the pieces of the puzzle. When the puzzle is complete, he gets that prize. Every time we did it with my kids, they pushed me out the door, wanting to get just a bit closer to their treasure."

"That's a great idea!" I said, excited to try it with Michael.

PRACTICE

Are your kids giving you a hard time for going out of town or leaving for meetings? Try the puzzle game. Remember, you don't have to go overboard on the prize. For kids, part of the fun is the process. Not only do they get a gift at the end, they also get to be part of your life.

Here are the steps:

- Buy two pieces of large poster board (the second is to be used as the backboard).
- Draw your kid's prize on one of the pieces of poster board. Let them color it in.
- Cut the sheet into as many pieces as you think is appropriate.
- Let them glue one piece on.
- Explain the rules to them. Every time you have to do **X** activity, they get to glue another piece.
- Game on!

NOTES

NOTES

CHAPTER 10
TIME FOR LOVE?

I introduced Michael to Sandy's puzzle game and he ate it up. He was so excited about getting the video game system he'd been begging me for. Luckily, I'd brought the poster board home from work, and we set about drawing the prize and cutting it into pieces right away.

We stuck it up on the wall in our kitchen, right next to our vision board, where Michael could see it throughout the day. The next morning, I found him in the darkened kitchen, sitting on the floor with his blanky, staring up at the mostly empty puzzle. He looked up and said, "Can you go now, Mommy, so I can put a piece on?" He had the piece in hand. I laughed and crushed him a bear hug. He squirmed until I put him down. I barely made it out the door with a banana, Michael pushing me the whole way.

+++

Weeks went by and Michael got closer and closer to completing his puzzle. There was still the occasional complaint about me leaving, but for the most part he settled in on his goal.

I did the same. My business took on a life of its own, to the point that I had to hire one of my friends to do part time administrative work. I'd grown my budding business larger than I had during its first iteration years before. A steady income, though still small, started hitting my bank account. It motivated me to do more. I kept Sandy apprised of my progress via email. She offered the occasional pointer, but mostly congratulated me and told me to call if I needed anything.

Managing my time became an obsession. Every night I reviewed my schedule for the next day, ensuring I was ready, scheduling more, setting appropriate time aside for my son. By then, I started thinking seriously about cutting back my hours at the hospital. Being able to look at my schedule so clearly and knowing how much I could accomplish within certain time frames showed me that with an extra six hours per week I could get a lot done in my business.

The next Monday I told my nurse manager that I wanted to rearrange my schedule a bit. She said that wouldn't be a problem and asked when I'd like to start.

"How about next week?"

"That works."

+++

On the way home, I stopped to put gas in my car. As I reached to put my credit card in the machine, I heard someone call my name.

"Erika!"

I turned around, not recognizing the voice. A man was walking my way from the little store, carrying a plastic bag. As he came closer, recognition clicked in my head. He'd lived in our old neighborhood, but I couldn't remember his name.

"Hello," I said cautiously.

"Hey. You don't remember me, do you?" He had a nice smile.

I blushed. "Sure, you lived in our neighborhood. I'm sorry, I don't remember your name."

He actually laughed. "That's okay. I wouldn't think someone like _you_ would remember someone like _me_," he said, grinning.

I blushed harder. It'd been a while since anyone had flirted with me.

"I'm Sean." He reached out a hand and I shook it, noticing its warmth.

"Good to see you again, Sean."

"Likewise. Hey how's your..."

"Husband?"

He nodded.

"We've been divorced for a few years," I said.

"I'm sorry."

"It's okay. We're still friends."

"That's cool. Well, um..." He kicked his foot against the curb and avoided my gaze. "Do you think...would you like to grab a coffee or something, sometime, I mean, you don't have to, but..."

I smiled at his unease. He was good-looking.

"Let me check my calendar," I said, matter-of-factly.

He looked up in surprise. "Isn't that what they say in the movies when the girl's gonna turn the guy down?"

I laughed and shook my head. "Maybe, but that's not me. I'm just really busy." I stuck my arm into the driver's side window and pulled out my organizer.

"You weren't kidding," he said.

I smiled. "How about Saturday?"

PRACTICE

Don't worry. We're not going to tell you to go out and look for the love of your life. You may have already found that person.

We will say that it's important to have someone in your life. A special person who will love you, and someone you can love in return. That person will usually show up when you least expect it.

If you haven't found love, keep your eyes and ears open, but don't stress it. A funny thing happens when you chase success. You become a magnet for great things, including love. Be open to it.

If you're already married, engaged or dating, cherish the person you're with. Schedule time to be with your husband. Be in the moment when you're with your girlfriend. As we've mentioned before, include them in your hopes and dreams. Ask about theirs. Together, on a united mission, you can do amazing things.

NOTES

NOTES

CHAPTER 11
MY TIME. MY LIFE.

It's been almost two years since I met Sandy in the hospital cafeteria. We still have coffee every couple months. She's busy and so am I.

I am eternally grateful for her friendship. There's not a day that goes by that I don't thank God for bringing her into my life. Because of my wonderful mentor, I've realized my dreams and my potential. I am special. I've created a new normal that fits my life. My family dreams with me. We're on our way. I even found love along the long road, literally.

I'm so blessed. Here are other lessons I've learned that I might not have mentioned before:

- Nothing compares to hard work.
- Hard work is great, but <u>smart</u> hard work is better.
- Smile often.

- Don't take yourself too seriously.
- Take your dreams very seriously.
- Be honest yet polite.
- Be honest with yourself.
- Sacrifice in order to have that which you desire.
- Don't sacrifice everything. Find balance.
- Don't listen to what the world thinks is normal. Make your own normal.
- If you believe in your dream, there are no other options.
- Have "me" time to recenter and refocus.
- Scheduled date nights are a must.
- Find a mentor.

Thank you so much for listening to my story. It's amazing how far I've come. Sometimes I don't like to think of the person I was before. We all go through ups and downs, but it's how we hop up and dust ourselves off that really counts, right?

Well, I've gotta run. Business is booming and today I'm interviewing a couple people to find a full-time personal assistant. I'm only working one day a week at the hospital, focusing on my business the rest of the time. I don't work much on the weekends anymore. Can you believe it? It's hard for me to wrap my head around. The other nurses look at me like I'm crazy, although I can tell most of them want the same thing. I even had one of my co-workers ask me if I needed any part-time help. We'll see.

I almost forgot! Michael and I finally got to go to Disney World last week. We stayed all week, and my mom got to come along, too. I think she's finally a believer. She helps me with paperwork sometimes.

Well, that's it for now. I wish you all the best. Remember, keep your eye on the prize. Don't let anyone steal your dreams. If I can do it, so can you.

NOTES

NOTES

We hope you've enjoyed Erika's story. If you did, **please leave an honest review**.

If you'd like to connect with Bethany, please visit http://BethanyWebster.com.

To see all the books in The Mentor Code series, and find out about new releases, please visit http://TheMentorCode.com.

For more information on author C. G. Cooper, please visit http://CarlosCooper.com.

www.ingramcontent.com/pod-product-compliance
Lightning Source LLC
Chambersburg PA
CBHW020928180526
45163CB00007B/2930